Florida Divorce: Getting Through the Monetary & Emotional Effects of Divorce

Daniel Ohm, Esq.

DEDICATION

To my Mother and Father who pushed me to go to law school and pushed me to strive to my full potential and to Jenna, without her I would have never been able to accomplish all of this.

CONTENTS

CHAPTER 1
SO YOU ARE THINKING OF GETTING DIVORCED

So you are thinking about getting divorced. Do not worry, you are not alone. Although divorce rates are falling in the United States, so are marriage rates. According to the Forest Institute of Professional Psychology, 45% to 50% of marriages will end in divorce. More stark news is that we as humans do not statistically improve by getting married more than once. We actually end up doing worse with each go around. On second marriages, the statistics skyrocket to 60% to 67% and third marriages are at 70% to 73%. Those are quite grim statistics. These are the statistics in the United States. Florida itself is ranked one of the highest divorce rates in the United States, with 13.1% of its population being divorcees in 2013.

With that level of divorce and the nature of my profession, I have seen my fair share of divorces in my lifetime. The one quandary I have always had with newly divorcees is that I never know whether to congratulate or send a sympathy card. I have learned that it greatly varies by individual. For some, divorce can be a blessing. For others it can be the equivalent of losing a loved one. Divorce is comprised of many complex emotions. I have seen people flourish after a divorce and come back better than ever. On the opposite side I have seen people get divorced and sink into deep depression and misery.   There is one constant though that never changes about people experiencing divorce:

IT IS NEVER PREDICTABLE HOW A DIVORCE WILL AFFECT SOMEONE UNTIL THEY ARE KNEE DEEP.

Divorce is not only emotionally draining, it can also be physically draining. The average cost of divorce in the United States is $15,000. For most Americans that is a steep price tag for a divorce.

WHO IS THIS BOOK FOR?

This book is for the individual who is thinking about filing for divorce, has already filed for divorce or has been served with divorce papers by a spouse. This book is intended to give you a summary overview of the divorce process, help you with emotional and monetary problems and help you get through your divorce as unscathed as possible. This book focuses on a relatively new process of divorce known as Collaborative Divorce. The purpose of this process of divorce is to resolve any issues that may arise in the divorce proceeding as amicably as possible and without court interference. This book covers the issues that should be covered and in what order, based on the acronym PEACE. PEACE is how and in what order the courts deal with the issues concerning divorce. PEACE stands for Parental Responsibility, equitable distribution, alimony, child support and everything else.

I suggest that you read this book in consecutive order at least once. This will allow you to get familiar with the emotional and legal issues concerning divorce. Once you have read the book you can go back to the sections that are most important to your individual situation. Many times I have had clients discover issues that they did not even know they had.

Last but not least, if you find yourself lost in your divorce proceeding, hire an attorney. I have seen many people who have come to me after a divorce, disgruntled about something in their agreement, that they had not even thought about at the time and I have not been able to help them change it. If at any time you have an issue you are unsure about, I implore you to find an attorney in your area. This can be the difference from an agreement you are happy with to an agreement that can haunt you later.

Also, this book is intended to give a brief overview of collaborative divorce proceedings; it is in no way a complete treatise on the subject. A complete treatise would be a much bigger book!

CHAPTER 2
FLORIDA DIVORCE LAW

The only requirement under Florida law to get a divorce is to prove that your marriage is 'Irretrievably Broken'. Under Florida Law either party may file for the dissolution of marriage by use of a petition. In the petition you must prove that the marriage legally exists, one of the parties has been a Florida resident for at least six months before filing the petition and the marriage is irretrievably broken.

Florida law has completely done away with 'Fault Divorces'. Florida does not require one spouse to prove the fault of the other in order to get a divorce. Fault of one spouse for the divorce holds very little relevance to dissolution proceedings. The only aspect that fault plays in Florida is when it comes to determining alimony.

There are two types of Divorces in Florida. These are simplified dissolution of marriage and regular dissolution of marriage. In a simplified dissolution of marriage all of the following requirements must be met:

• You and your spouse agree that the marriage cannot be saved.

• You and your spouse have no minor or dependent child(ren) together, the wife does not have any minor or dependent children born during the marriage, and the wife is not now pregnant.

• You and your spouse have worked out how the two of you will divide the things that you both own (your assets) and who will pay what part of the money you both owe (your liabilities), and you are both satisfied with this division.

•   You are not seeking support (alimony) from your spouse, and vice versa.

•   You and your spouse have filed financial affidavits with the court or you have waived the filing of financial affidavits and you are satisfied with the financial disclosure received from the other spouse.

•   You are willing to give up your right to trial and appeal.

•   You and your spouse are both willing to go into the clerk's office to sign the petition (not necessarily together).

•   You and your spouse are both willing to go to the final hearing (at the same time).

If you do not meet a single one of these requirements you are not eligible for a simplified divorce and you must file for a regular dissolution of marriage.

In a regular dissolution of marriage one side files the correct petition with the court. There are three petitions available for regular dissolution of marriage. They are:

• Petition for Dissolution of Marriage with Dependent or Minor Child(ren)

• Petition for Dissolution of Marriage with Property but No Dependent or Minor Child(ren)

• Petition for Dissolution of Marriage with No Dependent or Minor Child(ren) or Property

All the forms that you will need for your divorce can be found for free at: http://www.flcourts.org/resources-and-services/family-courts/family-law-self-help-information/family-law-forms.stml.

When filing a regular petition for the dissolution of marriage the filing spouse must ensure his or her partner is notified of the divorce proceeding. The notified spouse then has 20 days to respond.

Within 45 days of being notified that one spouse is seeking a divorce, the court will require discovery. Both sides must provide various financial documents. Care must be taken to provide complete and accurate information.

The main difference between an uncontested divorce and a contested divorce is a matter of time. While an uncontested divorce may be concluded within a few weeks, disagreements in a contested divorce can drag the proceeding out for months and even years. If the spouses cannot come to an agreement, their case will be heard by a judge, who will make the final decision.

CHAPTER 3
COLLABORATIVE DIVORCE

There is a new legal phenomenon occurring in the realm of divorce. This new legal phenomenon is called Collaborative Divorce. A Collaborative Divorce is a means of resolving your divorce, through compromise and negotiation, without having to go to court.

Now you may be asking, Dan, how is this different from going to mediation? Well, a collaborative divorce is a group effort. In a collaborative divorce, both parties retain separate attorneys, and commit to working together to come to a mutually beneficial agreement, and thus avoiding having a judge make the decisions.

In a collaborative divorce, the question is always, 'what is best for us?', whereas in mediation it is always, 'what is best for me?'.

So what are the benefits of having a collaborative divorce? There are many. To start collaborative divorces tend to be much less expensive then contested divorces. Also, each party tends to have a much greater degree of control in their divorce proceeding. Many do not like leaving the important issues for a judge to decide. Collaborative Divorce also allows for flexibility. It allows you to create a creative agreement that will work best for you and/or your family.

Sounds great you say! How do I go about getting a collaborative divorce you ask? The first step is for your spouse and you to find separate attorneys practicing collaborative divorce. Once both of you retain attorneys, the collaborative divorce will begin once both you and your spouse sign a 'Participation Agreement'. The 'Participation Agreement' lays out that the spouses will negotiate fairly and civilly. Although the 'Participation Agreements' will vary greatly from attorney to attorney, all 'Participation Agreements' will have a provision that the attorneys will exercise their best effort to come to a settlement and that they will withdraw from representation if the collaborative divorce fails and litigation ensues.

There may be many people in the collaborative divorce group. Some people that may be included in the group in order to come to a fair divorce settlement may be financial and tax advisors, mental health professionals, and accountants.

So what happens if the Collaborative Divorce process fails to work for you? If the Collaborative Divorce process fails for you, you are always left with the option of pursuing the dissolution of marriage through the court system. However, both parties will need to hire new attorneys to represent them.

CHAPTER 4
DIVORCE AND CHILDREN

One of the most difficult aspects of divorce is telling your children about it. How the divorce will affect them is the most common concern with parents. Your children will be affected from the divorce. There are steps you can take that will minimize the negative effects divorce may have on them.

Both parents should agree in advance about questions and answer of the how, when and, where, why. If the parents cannot agree to the answers, they should seek professional therapeutic advice and agree to follow that advice. Both parents should tell the child together and all children should be told at the same time.

Here are some tips to telling your children about divorce:

1. Offer clear and honest explanations as to the reason for the divorce. Avoid elaborate details of your marital problems or assigning blame.

2. Focus on telling what will happen to each child. Describe basic changes (i.e. living arrangements, financial changes, time with the other parent).

3. Assure your child he/she will be told of all major developments and changes.

4. Extend an invitation to your child to make suggestions that will be considered.

5. Stress that your child is not responsible for the dissolution of marriage, but that this is an issue between the adults. Emphasize that it is not the child's fault.

6. Reassure your child that the dissolution does not weaken the bond between the parent and the child.

7. Give your child permission to love both parents.

8. Assure the child that both parents love the child.

9. Give your child a time frame of the dissolution and expected changes.

10. Give your child a clear sense of an established place in each parent's home (i.e. their own room, place for toys, toiletries).

11. Impart that this is an adult decision and nothing the child does or can do can change this.

12. Tell children there are counselors with whom the child can consult confidentially with questions and help in addition to the parents; that the parents are also getting counseling to help. It is okay to need help and get help.

All children, regardless of age may show negative signs due to the divorce. This is completely normal. The following are some common reactions to divorce based on age:

- Infant to 3 years old
    - Most Affected?
        - Dependent
    - Least Affected?
        - Too young to witness conflict
    - Separation Anxiety from Primary caretaker
- 3 Years old to 5 ½ years old
    - Regressive Behavior
    - Fear of abandonment
    - Sadness

- o Whining
- 5 ½ Years old to 8 years old
  - o Sadness
  - o Crying
  - o Fear of abandonment
  - o Intense yearning for absent parent
  - o Aggression
  - o Feeling torn
- 9 Years old to 12 years old
  - o Intense Anger toward the parent wanting divorce.
  - o Identification with the "victim" parent
  - o Somatic symptoms
  - o School problems
- Teenagers
  - o Anguish
  - o Depression
  - o Anger
  - o Loyalty Conflicts
  - o Preoccupation with the future

o   School problems.

Certain things can be done in order to minimize these feelings. With children from infancy to 3 years old, it is important to create consistency, continuity, familiarity and stability. With children ages 3 years old to 5 ½ years old it is important to create predictability, consistency, clear and specific scheduling and stability. From 5 ½ years old to 8 years old, parents to give them attention and time, reassurance of love, adjustment times and shield them from conflict. With children ages 9 to 12, parents should create stability, shield the child away from conflict, allow the child to love both parents and set responsible and recreational time. With teenagers it is important to set boundaries, time sharing should be predictable and consistent, practice safe nurturing and set a positive example.

CHAPTER 5
EMOTIONAL STAGE OF DIVORCE

Before we start this chapter, I need to tell you something extremely important... Over time, things will improve. The onset might be bad, but over time and with a little work everyone can recover from the negative effects of a divorce. That being said, psychologists have determined that there are four major stages people go through during a divorce. The stages are:

- Stage 1: Shock and Disbelief
- Stage 2: Initial Adjustment

- Stage 3: Active Reorganization
- Stage 4: Life Reformation

Within Stage 1, there are 6 stages of grief that one will go through. These are:

- Shock
- Denial
- Anger
- Bargaining
- Depression
- Acceptance

People in the grieving stages tend to shift back and forth between the various stages of grief. Therefore, the grief stages can only be described in general terms. This is completely normal. It is important to be aware of the stages of grieving and determining which stage of the grieving process you are in. If you find yourself stuck in any of the stages for too long, you should consider counseling to help you get through the process. Unfortunately, the only cure for getting through the grieving stages is the passage of time.

Once you have gained acceptance of the divorce and gotten past Stage 1, Shock and Disbelief, it is time for Stage 2, initial adjustment. The primary goal in this stage is to adapt and gather the personal resources you'll need to manage the emotional and practical changes divorce brings. Stage 2 is all about practicality, managing your emotions and proceeding through the legal aspects of your divorce.

Stage 3, Active Reorganization, concerns the way you are living your life and accepting the enduring changes. You are now suddenly single, maybe even a single parent. This stage is all about redefining yourself and your life. During this stage you are redefining your lifestyle and relationships.

The final stage, Stage 4, Lifestyle Reformation, represents the last step of the emotional stages of divorce. Once you have reached this stage, the worst is behind you, and you have the opportunity to build your new life. At this stage it is all about starting anew. It is time to construct new relationships, find new interests, and most importantly accept your new life.

CHAPTER 6

REDUCING THE CHAOS OF DIVORCE

Face it, Divorce is chaotic. Many changes are coming about very quickly. These changes may include, change of residence, parenting, self-perception, social relationships, etc. This chaos can be harmful and lead to serious problems such as alcohol and drug abuse. The following is advice to get through your divorce with the least amount of chaos possible.

In order to limit the amount of chaos it is important to do the following:

- Limit the Amount of Changes in Your Life
- Protect Your Family
- Protect Your Financial Situation

Limit the Amount of Changes in Your Life

Change is what causes chaos in the first place it would be prudent to limit any dramatic changes in your life. The best rule of thumb is making no major changes in your life for at least a period of one year. Through the years, I have seen numerous people going through a divorce make drastic changes that they later regret. So before you sell all your material possessions and join a commune, put it on hold for one year. There are enough changes going on in your life, don't add anymore.

Another mistake people often make during and after a divorce is getting into another relationship too quickly. This creates all kinds of problems and conflicts. While you are going through a divorce, and for a short period thereafter you are extremely vulnerable. Any relationship you enter into will be based on panic, need, or grief. This is not a healthy relationship and will only lead to problems. Also, entering into a relationship too quickly can lead to a jealous ex-spouse. This can lead to problems in negotiating the divorce and violence concerns.

Protect Your Family

During this time the most important people you can protect are your children. Throughout the divorce proceedings they should come first. It is important to make sure they have what they need. It is your job to shelter your children from the effects of the divorce. Always maintain a positive attitude around your children. The divorce will already have them stressed and it should be your duty to shelter them from this stress. Focusing on your children will also have a beneficial effect on you as well. Focusing on your children keeps you from dwelling on the problems that you are currently facing.

Members of your family can be your greatest allies. It is important not to alienate them in this stressful situation. Be careful not to take out your issues on them. Your family will be there to support and defend you every step of the way. Your family can be your biggest source of strength, respect them.

You should also respect your spouse, especially if you have children. Respecting your spouse will allow you to get through your divorce in an amicable way most of the time. If bitterness and hatred rule the contact with your spouse you will almost certainly hit many speed bumps along the way. If you and your spouse have children, you will be parents forever. This means whether you like it or not you will have to have some sort of relationship with your spouse after the divorce. You must be able to put your anger aside and avoid labeling your spouse as the enemy for the sake of your children.

Protect Your Financial Situation

Protect your job, it is more important than it has even been before. Bringing in the issues of your divorce into work could jeopardize your job. Talk to your employer about your situation. Do whatever you need to do to keep your work relationship healthy. You may be unhappy with your job, this may be due to the divorce. If after a year you are still unhappy begin looking for a new job. Make sure you give proper notice and don't burn any bridges.

Another common result of divorce is excessive spending on unnecessary things. Make sure you pay your bills. Make sure the necessities of life for you and your children come first. Make sure any money you have goes to protect people, then assets and finally your credit rating.

CHAPTER 7

PARENTAL RESPONSIBILITY

The Florida legislature has replaced the term custody and visitation with parental responsibility, primary residential responsibility, secondary parental responsibility and time sharing. Florida Statute Section 61.13(2)(b)1 states that:

It is the public policy of this state to assure that each minor child has frequent and continuing contact with both parents after the parents separate or the marriage of the parties is dissolved and to encourage parents to share the rights and responsibilities of childrearing. After considering all relevant facts, the father of the child shall be given the same consideration as the mother in determining the primary residence of a child irrespective of the age or the sex of the child.

Florida Statute Section 61.13(2)(b)(2) states that "the court shall order that the parental responsibility for a minor child be shared by both parents unless the court finds that shared parental responsibility would be detrimental to the child."

If for some reason you and your spouse cannot agree how time sharing of the children will go, the judge must decide the question of custody. The judge will consider the following factors:

- Which parent is most likely to follow the time sharing schedule and develop and maintain a close parent-child relationship

- Love, affection and other emotional ties existing between the child and each parent
- Ability of each parent to provide the children with food, clothing, medical care and other needs.
- Length of time the child has lived with either parent
- The permanence of the proposed custodial home.
- Moral fitness of each parent
- Mental and physical health of each parent
- Home, school and community record of the children
- The preference of the child
- Any other relevant factors

Visitation is the time a child spends with the parent who does not have primary parental responsibility. Visitation could be anywhere from a few hours to the entire summer vacation.

In determining parental responsibility, the court will approve the parenting plan developed by you and your spouse. If you cannot come to an arrangement, the court will devise a parenting plan for you. A parenting plan includes who will take responsibility for the daily tasks of the child rearing, a time-sharing schedule and who will have decision making authority related to health care and school.

The key to drafting a visitation schedule is flexibility. You and your spouse should be able to make adjustments to the schedule and should agree to do so. Things come up; you should arrange a visitation schedule that allows for flexibility in things that come up in life.

Not being able to agree on these matters can prove to be problematic. Any matter you and your spouse cannot agree on will be decided by a judge. Unfortunately, the judge does not know your child, you or your spouse. Leaving such an important family decision to a complete stranger can force a bad arrangement.

In very rare cases, the court can order sole parental responsibility to one parent. In order for a court to order sole parental responsibility to one parent, the court must find that shared parental responsibility would be detrimental to the child. Drug and alcohol abuse is the most common argument against a spouse for shared parental responsibility. Unless there is an arrest or conviction it is quite difficult though, to prove. It is usually a poor idea to accuse your spouse with being unfit unless there is good proof. Judges tend

to anger over unfounded allegations against a
spouse.

CHAPTER 8
EQUITABLE DISTRIBUTION

Florida statute provides for equitable distribution of marital assets (property) and liabilities (debt). Florida law calls for a division of the assets and debts of the marriage *fairly*. *Fairly* does not mean equal. Assets and debts are separated into two categories: marital property and nonmarital property.

In determining the difference between marital property and nonmarital property apply the following:

- If the asset or debt was acquired after the date of your marriage, there is a presumption that it is marital property

- If the asset or debt was acquired before the date of your marriage there is a presumption that it is nonmarital property. It is also nonmarital property if you acquired it through a gift or inheritance.

Marital assets and debts acquired during your marriage are still marital property even though you or your spouse acquired it individually. Also, all rights received during the marriage such as, a pension, retirement plan, profit-sharing, and insurance are marital property.

The increase in the value of a nonmarital asset during the marriage, or the use of marital funds to pay for or improve the property is marital property. If nonmarital property is given to the other spouse it thereby becomes marital property.

CHAPTER 9
ALIMONY

In Florida, either the husband or the wife may receive alimony. Courts look at need and ability to pay in determining whether to award alimony. There are four types of alimony:

- Rehabilitative Alimony

- Permanent Alimony

- Lump Sum Alimony

*   Bridge-the-Gap Alimony

Rehabilitative Alimony

Rehabilitative alimony is for a limited period of time. Its purpose is to enable the spouse to get education or training that would be necessary to redevelop skills and financial independence in order to find a job. In order to qualify for Rehabilitative alimony there must be a rehabilitation plan.

Permanent Alimony

This type of alimony continues for a long time, possibly until the death of the parties receiving the alimony. This type of alimony is usually given when one party is unable to work due to age, physical illness or mental illness.

Lump Sum Alimony

This is a fixed sum alimony. It is payable either all at once or in installments.

This can be paid either by money or property. Lump sum alimony is more similar to property division then actual alimony.

Bridge-the-Gap Alimony

The purpose of Bridge-the-Gap Alimony is to assist one spouse in making the transition from a marital to a single state.

In determining what type of alimony to award, the courts consider the following factors:

- The standard of living during the marriage
- Length of the marriage
- Age, physical, and emotional conditions of each party
- Financial resources of each party
- Contribution of each party to the marriage
- Any other relevant economic factors

When negotiating for a settlement, waiver of alimony is not recommended. Nominal alimony should be requested in order to reserve the right to collect alimony later. If the reservation for alimony is not requested it cannot be awarded later. Also, as an alternative to alimony, you may want to negotiate for a larger portion of property instead of alimony payments.

CHAPTER 10

CHILD SUPPORT

Anytime a divorce involves children under the age of eighteen, child support will become an issue. Both parents have a responsibility to support their minor children. Child support is a right belonging to the children. Parents cannot contract away child support in a settlement agreement. This support is based on the child's needs and the parent's income level. Some of the most important issues that arise concerning child support are:

- The method child support will be paid
- Ways payment can be assured
- When Child Support can be increased or decreased
- Who will get the dependency deduction on the yearly taxes

The Amount of Child Support

Florida has guidelines to determine who will pay what in terms of child support. Family Law Form 12.902(e) which can be found at http://www.flcourts.org/core/fileparse.php/293/urlt/902e.pdf, helps you calculate child support for you and your spouse and determines who will pay for the child support. The guidelines calculate a child support payment based on income and the number of children. Adjustments are made to this number based on the number of substantial overnight stays with a parent.

Rough calculations for child support equal to the following:

- One Child- 22% of net income
- Two Children- 32% of net income
- Three Children- 41% of net income

The Court has ultimate authority when it comes to child support. The Court may order child support which varies from what you have decided with your spouse. They cannot however stray from the guideline amount of more than 5% without good cause. Some of the factors considered by the Courts when reviewing the guideline amounts are:

- Needs of the children
- Age of the children
- Standard of living
- Financial status of both parents
- Ability of both parents

The Method Child Support Will Be Paid

Child Support may be paid by direct or indirect payments. Direct payments are self-explanatory, but indirect payments can include mortgage payments, insurance, etc. Direct payments should be paid by the Florida Child Support Depository. The Florida Child Support Depository or similar depository for your jurisdiction. By paying child support through a depository allows the court to keep a record of all paid child support.

Ways Payment Can Assured

There are many ways that payment of child support can be assured. Not paying child support can have serious consequences such as, wage garnishment, suspension or denial of professional licenses and certificates, suspension of Driver's License, vehicle registration, and jail time. Not paying child support is never recommended. If you or your spouse is unable to pay for the current child support, modification is recommended.

Suspending child support payments is never the answer.

Although child support ends upon the death of the paying party, life insurance policies can be sought in order to secure financial stability in the event of death.

When Child Support Can Be Increased or Decreased

Once child support is set, there is only one criteria that will allow for a modification of child support. This criteria is a substantial change in circumstances. For example, an increase or decrease in income or a change in the child's needs.

It should be noted that throughout any of these court proceedings, one cannot be voluntarily unemployed or underemployed in order to decrease child support payments. Courts tend to not take kindly to this kind of behavior. If a court finds that a parent is unemployed or underemployed voluntarily, absent physical or mental incapacity, the court will impute income on the parent. *Impute income* means that the court will assign a value to infer what a parent should be making based on a number of factors. These factors are:

- Recent work history
- Occupational qualifications
- Prevailing earning level in the community

Who Will Get The Dependency Deduction on the Yearly Taxes

As if things aren't stressful enough, you and your spouse need to discuss who will claim income tax deductions for expenses related to your children. If you both claim the same deductions on your taxes, you both are at serious risk for an IRS audit.

With the passage the Affordable Health Care act, the general rule has become that the parent who provides the health insurance for the child, will be entitled to claim the child as a dependent on the taxes.

This is an issue that you should discuss with your accountant or financial advisor to determine what is the best strategy when it comes to the dependency deduction.

Chapter 11

EVERYTHING ELSE

So who gets the TV and who gets the appliances during the divorce? Divorces that get down to the nitty-gritty are a losing game. The Court is not interested in dividing petty things. Although the material items may be important to you or your spouse, the Courts simply do not care to rule on such things.

Whenever you and your spouse are fighting over material items, it is often helpful to do a cost/benefit analysis. Is what you are fighting for worth the monetary and emotional turmoil?

I have seen countless clients arguing for the silliest of things. Most of the time it simply comes down to the fact that they may not want the item, but they especially do not want their spouse to have the item. I tend to find these things petty and will often tell my clients that it just simply is not worth arguing over. Try to avoid arguing over the petty items that were accumulated during your marriage. Your divorce as well as your mental sanity will go a whole lot smoother.

ABOUT THE AUTHOR

Daniel Ohm, Esq. was born in South Florida. He went to school for his undergrad at Wilkes Honors College at Florida Atlantic University. After graduation he attended Florida Coastal School of Law where he received his law degree.

www.ingramcontent.com/pod-product-compliance
Lightning Source LLC
Chambersburg PA
CBHW021443170526
45164CB00001B/367